Food Field Trips

T0021065

Let's Explore
Strawberries!

Jill Colella

Lerner Publications ◆ Minneapolis

Hello, Friends,

Everybody eats, even from birth. This is why learning about food is important. Making the right choice about what to eat begins with knowing more about food. Food literacy helps us to be more curious about food and adventurous about what we eat. In short, it helps us discover how delicious the world of food can be.

One of my favorite foods to eat is strawberries. I love to eat strawberries for dessert. I like mine sliced, in a bowl, and topped with a little dollop of whipped cream.

For more inspiration, ideas, and recipes, visit www.teachkidstocook.com.

Jill

About the Author
Happy cook, reformed picky eater, and longtime classroom teacher Jill Colella founded both *Ingredient* and *Butternut*, award-winning children's magazines that promote food literacy.

Lerner Publications Company
An imprint of Lerner Publishing Group, Inc.
241 First Avenue North
Minneapolis, MN 55401 USA

For reading levels and more information, look up this title at www.lernerbooks.com.

Main body text set in Mikado. Typeface provided by HVD.

Library of Congress Cataloging-in-Publication Data

Names: Colella, Jill, author.
Title: Let's explore strawberries / by Jill Colella.
Description: Minneapolis, MN : Lerner Publications, [2020] | Series: Food field trips | Includes bibliographical references and index.
Identifiers: LCCN 2019011839 (print) | LCCN 2019013925 (ebook) | ISBN 9781541582989 (eb pdf) | ISBN 9781541563025 (lb : alk. paper)
Subjects: LCSH: Cooking (Strawberries)—Juvenile literature.
Classification: LCC TX813.S9 (ebook) | LCC TX813.S9 C65 2020 (print) | DDC 641.6/475—dc23

LC record available at https://lccn.loc.gov/2019011839

Manufactured in the United States of America
1-46464-47541-6/26/2019

SCAN FOR BONUS CONTENT!

Table of Contents

Picture Glossary

berry

fruit

jam

patch

ripe

ALL ABOUT STRAWBERRIES

Strawberries are a tasty fruit. Sweet like candy, they are yummy to eat alone.

You can add strawberries to foods such as yogurt, salad, or cereal. Or add them to desserts.

Strawberries grow in the spring and summer. Some people make them into jam or jelly to enjoy all year long.

LET'S COMPARE

Berries come in different shapes, sizes, and colors. Some berries are sweet, and some are sour. Which taste do you like better?

Which berries are the same color? How
many of these berries have you tried?
Do you have a favorite?

strawberry

blackberry

raspberry

blueberry

gooseberry

black
currant

LET'S EXPLORE

When is a berry ripe? A ripe fruit or vegetable is ready to eat. Strawberries begin tiny and green. They are not yet ripe. They grow larger and turn red. Then they are ready to pick and eat!

Which of these strawberries are ripe?

LET'S VISIT A BERRY FARM

Strawberries grow in fields on a farm.
A field of strawberry plants is a patch.

The plants grow in long rows. Their tops are green and leafy. They are crowns.

Why do you think the green, leafy top is called a crown?

Pull back the leaves. Do you see the berries growing underneath?

The strawberries are different colors. They are green, white, and red. Some are small, and others are big.

Small white and green berries aren't ripe yet. They are hard and sour.

What other foods get ripe before we eat them?

If you pick them, they will not turn ripe. A berry must ripen on the plant.

Pick a bright red berry from the plant, and put it in a basket. This berry is ripe and ready to eat.

How do you think a ripe berry tastes?

Keep looking to find
more ripe berries.
Slugs and bugs like
to eat berries too.

Do you see any
on the plants?

Look at the berries in your basket.
Which is the largest? The smallest?
The greenest? The reddest?

Wash your strawberries, and take a bite.
Eating berries is just as fun as picking them!

LET'S COOK

Smoothies make good breakfasts for busy mornings. This recipe makes 1 to 2 servings. Always remember to have an adult present when working in the kitchen!

STRAWBERRY SMOOTHIES

INGREDIENTS

- 8 strawberries, cleaned and hulled
- ½ cup (120 mL) milk
- 1 teaspoon vanilla
- ½ cup (125 g) vanilla yogurt
- 6 ice cubes

1. Put all ingredients in a blender.

2. With an adult's help, blend until smooth.

3. Pour into cups.

4. Put strawberries on the edge of your cup as a garnish.

5. Enjoy!

SEE THIS RECIPE IN ACTION!

LET'S MAKE

This recipe makes about
10 servings.

CHOCOLATE-COVERED FRUIT POPS

MATERIALS

- 4 ounces (112 g) chocolate, chopped

- 10 wooden skewers

- 10 strawberries, washed and dried

- 3 bananas, cut in chunks

- wax paper

- toppings (sprinkles, nuts, and candy-coated chocolate pieces)

1. An adult should put the chocolate in a glass bowl.

2. Microwave it for 30 seconds and stir. Microwave it for 30 more seconds. Repeat until the chocolate is melted and smooth.

3. Skewer the fruit and dip it in the chocolate. Lay it on wax paper.

4. Sprinkle with toppings.

5. Refrigerate until chocolate hardens.

6. Remove from refrigerator and enjoy!

Let's Read

All about Strawberries
http://www.produceforkids.com/produce-tips/strawberries

Just Ripe for You
http://ncstrawberry.com/about/kids

Owings, Lisa. *From Strawberry to Jam*. Minneapolis: Lerner Publications, 2015.

Pallotta, Jerry. *The Very Berry Counting Book*. Watertown, MA: Charlesbridge, 2017.

Schuh, Mari. *From Seed to Strawberry*. Minneapolis: Lerner Publications, 2017.

Index

Photo Acknowledgments

Image credits: hiramtom/E+/Getty Images, p. 1; Eduardo Gonzalez Diaz/EyeEm/Getty Images, p. 3 (jam); Phatcharee Saetoen/EyeEm/Getty Images, p. 3 (berry); npdesignde/iStock/Getty Images, p. 3 (patch); Michelle Arnold/EyeEm/Getty Images, p. 3 (fruit); Birte Möller/EyeEm/Getty Images, p. 3 (ripe); Sasiistock/iStock/Getty Images, p. 4; Anfisa Kameneva/EyeEm/Getty Images, p. 5 (top); Mizina/iStock/Getty Images, p. 5 (bottom left); Jamie Grill/Getty Images, p. 5 (bottom right); serezniy/iStock/Getty Images, p. 6; Carol Yepes/Getty Images, p. 7 (top); ArtMarie/E+/Getty Images, pp. 7 (bottom left), 16; WIRACHAIPHOTO/Shutterstock.com, p. 7 (bottom right); huayang/Moment/Getty Images, p. 8 (strawberry); mphillips007/E+/Getty Images, p. 8 (blackberry); lacaosa/Moment/Getty Images, p. 8 (raspberry); MirageC/Moment/Getty Images, p. 8 (blueberry); bruev/iStock/Getty Images, p. 8 (gooseberry); Henrik Sorensen/DigitalVision/Getty Images, p. 8 (black currant); Savushkin/iStock/Getty Images, p. 9 (top left); George-Standen/iStock/Getty Images, p. 9 (top right); TualekPhoto/Shutterstock.com, p. 9 (bottom left); YuriyS/iStock/Getty Images, pp. 9 (bottom right), 15; Ron and Patty Thomas/E+/Getty Images, p. 10; nikkytok/Shutterstock.com, p. 11 (top); Margarita Borodina/Shutterstock.com, p. 11 (bottom); miniloc/iStock/Getty Images, p. 12; sarintra chimphoolsuk/Shutterstock.com, p. 13 (top); PatrikStedrak/iStock/Getty Images, p. 13 (bottom); Yury Smelov/Shutterstock.com, p. 14 (top); BigKhem/Shutterstock.com, p. 14 (bottom); photowind/Shutterstock.com, p. 17 (top); Kyaw_Thiha/iStock/Getty Images, p. 17 (bottom); Beata Aldridge/EyeEm/Getty Images, p. 18; Inti St Clair/Getty Images, p. 19; bondvit/Shutterstock.com, p. 20; Laura Westlund/Independent Picture Service, pp. 20, 21, 22, 23 (illustrations); 10'000 Hours/DigitalVision/Getty Images, p. 21; holgs/E+/Getty Images, p. 22.

Cover: pixelheadphoto digitalskillet/Shutterstock.com (hands); Dream79/Shutterstock.com (jam); N.Minton/Shutterstock.com (strawberries); kazuya goto/Shutterstock.com (boy); Vincenzo Dato/Getty Images (back).